wake up

AWAKENING SERIES · VOLUME TWO

wake up

AN INTRODUCTION TO THE SECOND HALF OF THE GOSPEL

Mark Benjamin Matt LeRoy J. D. Walt

Printed in the United States of America

Cover and page design by Strange Last Name
Page layout by PerfecType, Nashville, Tennessee

Benjamin, Mark.
Wake up : an introduction to the second half of the gospel / Mark Benjamin, Matt LeRoy, J.D. Walt. – Frankin, Tennessee : Seedbed Publishing, ©2018. Second edition.

pages ; cm. – (Awakening series ; volume 2)

ISBN 9781628246353 (paperback)
ISBN 9781628246490 (Mobi)
ISBN 9781628246506 (ePub)
ISBN 9781628246513 (uPDF)

1. Devotional calendars. 2. Meditations. 3. Spiritual exercises. 4. Religious awakening--Christianity. I. Title. II. Series. III. LeRoy, Matthew. IV. Walt, John David.

BV4810.B46 2018   260   2018955899

SEEDBED PUBLISHING
Franklin, Tennessee
seedbed.com

CONTENTS

Why Discipleship Bands? vii
What Is a Discipleship Band? xi
What Do Discipleship Bands Do? xv
How to Use This Book xix

Week 1: Orientation 3

Week 2: Dissatisfied 13

Week 3: Deeper 25

Week 4: Dependent 37

Week 5: Delighted 49

Week 6: Devoted 61

The Discipleship Band Meeting Structure 72

why discipleship bands?

In his final hours, Jesus prayed specifically for us, "that all of them may be one, Father, just as you are in me and I am in you. May they also be in us so that the world may believe that you have sent me" (John 17:21).

Jesus prayed for the relationships between his followers to be of the very same character of the relationships between Father, Son, and Holy Spirit. Further, he prayed that our relationships would themselves find their home within the relationships of Father, Son, and Holy Spirit. Finally, note why this matters so much. Our relationships with each other will either lead people closer to God or further away.

Why discipleship bands? Because banded discipleship creates the context for the supernatural love of God to become real in our lives and through our relationships for the world. Discipleship bands all at once create space for inward transformation and outward mission.

The great tragedy of Christian discipleship is that it has come to mean so many things it can mean next to nothing. To be sure, there are complexities to discipleship, but at the core we must have deep clarity. In his final instructions to us, Jesus made it clear:

"All authority in heaven and on earth has been given to me. Therefore go and make disciples of all nations, baptizing them in the name of the Father and of the Son and of the Holy Spirit, and teaching them to obey everything I have commanded you. And surely I am with you always, to the very end of the age." (MATT. 28:18-20)

We are to make disciples and teach them to obey everything Jesus has commanded us.

Let's be clear. We are not talking about a new small-group program, or better accountability groups, or Bible study groups. We do not fail at the mission of God in the world for lack of more information or better content or enhanced skills. We fail for a lack of love. Our foremost challenge is not learning more but loving more.

We like the way our friend Phil Meadows describes discipleship bands:

A band is a form of fellowship that is a means of charismatic encounter with the presence, leading, and power of the Holy Spirit. We come together. Jesus Christ is present as he has promised and he breathes his Spirit powerfully. And we come to help one another fix our eyes on him, in our midst. And we come to help one another open wide our mouths to receive the Spirit he gives. And we come to have holy conversation.

The success of the gospel of Jesus Christ rises and falls on the strength of the relationships among his followers. Jesus' ambition was not to create a bunch of autonomous individual miracle workers. His mission is to create miraculous communities. This happens very simply through the arduous journey of people learning to love one another in the very same way that the Father and the Son and the Holy Spirit love one another.

There's nothing new here. It's actually quite ancient. From Jesus' band of disciples to the present day, everywhere the church has flourished some manner of banded discipleship was at the heart of it.

Most of us aren't lazy in our faith. We are stuck. It is not that we lack commitment. We are simply arrested in our development. The way forward is as close as a few other people who are willing to band together.

what is a
discipleship band?

A discipleship band is a group of three to five people who read together, pray together, and meet together to become the love of God for one another and the world.

Carefully consider this visionary text of Scripture from Paul's letter to the Ephesians.

> *I pray that out of his glorious riches he may strengthen you with power through his Spirit in your inner being, so that Christ may dwell in your hearts through faith. And I pray that you, being rooted and established in love, may have power, together with all the Lord's holy people, to grasp how wide and long and high and deep is the love of Christ, and to know this love that surpasses knowledge— that you may be filled to the measure of all the fullness of God.* (3:16-19)

First, note this is the Word of God. Second, it is a prayer. Third, it is all about relationships. For these reasons and more, it serves as a foundational text for our work. Discipleship bands provide a context where we can do these three things well. We read together. We pray together. We meet together. And we do these things with the all-consuming goal of being "filled to the measure of all the fullness of God." This is the way toward becoming the love of God for one another and the world.

WHY SO SMALL?

It's not that reading and praying and meeting can't happen in a larger group. The point of a discipleship band is the depth and quality of discipleship possible in a micro-community model. In truth, there are only so many people one can connect with on this level of intentionality. When it comes time to meet together, it is most effective to allot at least twenty minutes for each person (to share and be prayed for). In our experience, five member bands are not advisable; two-hour meetings become difficult to manage.

WHY SAME GENDER?

While sin is common to the human race, at times it takes on different character and qualities when it comes to different genders. Because of the way shame accompanies sin it can give rise to complicated dynamics between women and men. On the one hand, mixed gender groups can hinder vulnerability because of the presence of shame. On the other hand, vulnerable sharing can create inappropriate bonding. A discipleship band must be an ever-growing place of safety, where shame can be shed and truth can be told. Anything that tends to hinder this should be avoided. While mixed gender bands are permissible, in our judgment they are not advisable.

WHY SO SIMPLE?

Small groups satisfy many needs across the span of one's life. Discipleship bands provide a focused context for depth discipleship over a significant span of time. They aren't intended to be mission or service oriented. They aim to prepare people for mission by causing the mission of the gospel to become more deeply realized in one's own life.

Discipleship begins with understanding what God has done for us. It moves to God doing this work in us. Finally, it matures as God does this work through us in the world. Many programmatic models skip over the second phase, moving people from an understanding of what God has done for us to people doing something for God. The big challenge of discipleship centers around the work of God in us.

Because it's easier to measure and report outside activity, and because it is so difficult to measure the transformation of one's deepest self, and because there is so much desperate need all around us, it is tempting to skip the inside work and cut straight to the action part. Lest we establish a false dichotomy, let's be clear—discipleship is both inside and outside. The established tendency has been to skip the former to get to the latter, resulting in a brand of mission work that is helpful but shallow, well-intentioned but self-interested.

WHY SO DIFFICULT?

Most of us are arrested in our discipleship development. We get stuck repeating the same patterns of sin. We have believed lies about God and ourselves and they hold us like a prison with bars we can't see. Depth discipleship is hard because human beings have an unfortunate and almost infinite propensity to deceive themselves. The prophet Jeremiah said it best.

> *The human heart is the most deceitful of all things, and desperately wicked. Who really knows how bad it is?*
> (JER. 17:9 NLT)

Despite our best intentions, the reason we are stuck is we do not have the kinds of relationships it takes to catalyze and sustain the kind of work the Holy Spirit wills to do in our lives. This kind of soul work requires an ever-growing honesty with oneself; the kind of honesty that is next to impossible apart from a few other people alongside. It is why we must band together.

what do discipleship bands do?

1. Bands Read Together

The grass withers, the flower fades, but the word of our God will stand forever. (ISA. 40:8 ESV)

We are a people of One Book. The Word of God is both our constitution and compass. Though a discipleship band is not a Bible study group, one of the ways we band together is through reading a common text. John Wesley once famously wrote this stinging admonition in a letter to a certain Mr. John Premboth.

Whether you like it or not, read and pray daily. It is for your life; there is no other way; else you will be a trifler all your days, and a petty, superficial preacher. Do justice to your own soul; give it time and means to grow. Do not starve yourself any longer. Take up your cross and be a Christian altogether. Then will all children of God rejoice (not grieve) over you in particular.[1]

---

1 Taken from an editorial by J. B. Chapman in *The Preacher's Magazine* (vol. 6, no. 1, January 1, 1931). The note was written to John Premboth on August 17, 1760.

There are many ways to go about reading together. What matters is finding a way to get on the same page of Scripture together. Our common text does not function as the centerpiece of the band, rather it serves in a circumferential fashion to further band the group together.

2. Bands Pray Together

Devote yourselves to prayer, being watchful and thankful.
(COL. 4:2)

Our commitment is to watch over one another in love, to be for one another, and to encourage one another and build each other up. Our ongoing prayer life is a fundamental and foundational way we nurture these commitments. Band mates are prayer partners. We pray together in our weekly meeting, but even when we lift one another up throughout the week, we are, in effect, praying together. Over time band mates will know one another in extraordinary ways and will develop the capacity to pray for each other like few others in our lives can.

Every week in the band meeting, each person will have an opportunity to pray for another and to be prayed for. These times of prayer, perhaps more than anything else, will serve to strengthen the bonds of the band in deeply meaningful ways.

3. Bands Meet Together

Let us hold unswervingly to the hope we profess, for he who promised is faithful. And let us consider how we may spur one another on toward love and good deeds,

*not giving up meeting together, as some are in the habit
of doing, but encouraging one another—and all the more
as you see the Day approaching.* (HEB. 10:23-25)

A discipleship band has not banded together until it is regularly meeting together. Meeting together is the most critical component of the discipleship band experience. Finding a time when everyone can consistently meet together can be challenging, but in our experience, a consistent time each week works best.

Aim for four meetings a month, but you can settle for a minimum of three. If it slips to two, the meeting time should be reconsidered. This highlights the problem with setting a meeting frequency of less than weekly. Meetings inevitably get cancelled, and when this happens within a bi-weekly or monthly approach it hurts the efficacy of the band.

Meeting together can take on a variety of formats. Face-to-face is obviously the best option, but a video-chat or phone call also works fine. Some bands find themselves all living in different places, making a face-to-face meeting impossible. They meet by conference call or video-chat and work toward an annual in-person retreat together. The point is to do what works and whatever it takes.

*"Again, truly I tell you that if two of you on earth agree
about anything they ask for, it will be done for them by
my Father in heaven. For where two or three gather in my
name, there am I with them."* (MATT. 18:19-20)

how to use this book

You hold in your hands a resource designed specifically for a discipleship band. It facilitates the threefold work of a band to read together, pray together, and meet together. It is recommended for band members to read one of the entries each day, allowing it to guide your praying for one another and otherwise keep you reading a common text. Keep in mind, this is not meant to be a study curriculum proper. These readings are not meant to be the centerpiece of the weekly meeting but rather they are meant to keep a band on the same page throughout the week. Perhaps it will provide fodder for a group's informal interactions in any given week. Your band can elect to cover anywhere from five to seven readings per week at your own discretion.

On page 72 of this book you'll find a guide to conduct the discipleship band meeting, which you will find helpful as you meet together.

wake up

WEEK ONE
ORIENTATION

Note: For this first week, it seems best to give an orientation around the goal and aspiration of this resource. We can use each day to set the compass for where we are headed and carve out the rhythm for our journey together.

1. DISSATISFIED

READ

What good will it be for someone to gain the whole world, yet forfeit their soul? (MATT. 16:26)

REFLECT

Henry David Thoreau once famously said, "Most people lead lives of quiet desperation, and they go to the grave with the song still in them."

Quiet desperation. It could be the curse of our time. It is signaled by the all-too-common response to the question, "How are you doing?" "Fine," we answer. Someone once pointed out that the word *fine*, in this context, offers an apt acronym: Frustrated, Impatient, Nervous, and Exhausted. We manage this quiet desperation by smart phone and hold it at bay by a thousand small distractions. You know what I'm talking about, don't you?

One of two things will turn up the volume on this quiet desperation: crisis or awakening. And though it is not a requirement, often it takes the former to produce the latter. Either way, the beginning of awakening in our lives is signaled by a growing awareness of the gnawing dissatisfaction in the pit of our souls. Let's call it a holy dissatisfaction. To the extent we are not attuned to this reality we are still asleep.

True growth most often begins with a growing sense of dissonance. We are dissatisfied with the way things are. We are not the person we hoped we would become by now. Unheeded, this discontent can lead anywhere from a numbing affluence to a disastrous addiction. When we pay attention to this dissatisfaction it can lead to tremendous breakthroughs into the greater purposes for our lives. Paying attention means opening the vault of our quiet desperation and bringing forth our dissatisfaction, that it might be named aloud and offered to God.

PRAY

Heavenly Father, something deep down tells me there's more to this life than I presently know and experience. I do not want to settle for less than what you want for me. I want to trust you that underneath my discontent are your divine purposes, your dreams, and your plans for me. Come, Holy Spirit, and grant me the courage to turn away from all that would distract me, and grant me the grace to become completely honest with myself before you. And I pray this for (name your band mates). In Jesus' name, amen.

CONFERENCE

Can you begin to name the holy dissatisfaction in your life? Give it a try.

2. DEEPER

READ

For whoever wants to save their life will lose it,
but whoever loses their life for me will find it. (MATT. 16:25)

REFLECT

Deeper. Everybody wants to go deeper, but nobody wants to go down. Dissatisfaction will lead in one of two directions: distraction or depth. Deeper, contrary to popular belief, is not up. It's down. Deeper requires descent. This is the paradoxical journey of the gospel, which can be translated, "The way up is the way down." Jesus teaches us we find our life by losing it. The least is the greatest. The last is the first. The greatest is the servant of all. To go deeper does not mean to simply accept these truths as nice platitudes, rather it means to delve into the depths of them until their wisdom becomes miraculously evident to us. In fact, the only way to discover their truth is to descend into their reality.

Admittedly, the way to depth is a counterintuitive path. It requires faith. And remember, faith does not mean seeing is believing. Quite the opposite, faith means believing is seeing. Deeper opens the way to a new kind of wholeness. It is wellness as the well-known hymn states, "It is well with my soul." The journey is not an easy one. It requires navigation into our own broken ways. Yes, it will take courage to go there. It will lead to the unearthing of the lies we have believed and built on and the unraveling of the false selves we have constructed. The beauty of the journey of deeper is the ongoing unveiling of our truest and best selves—the people God intended when he first imagined us; even better, when he first imaged us.

Deeper is not another behavior or sin-management strategy. Deeper takes us into the realm of our dispositions, affections, and desires. Deeper leads to the discipleship of the heart and mind.

PRAY

Lord Jesus, thank you for not only showing the way to a life of true depth, but for taking us by the hand and leading us there. We confess, if left to us, we would plan a series of mountaintop moments filled with warm and fuzzy feelings. We know it means following you all the way to the cross and back again. Come, Holy Spirit, and fill us with the joy of going there together. We pray in your name, Jesus. Amen.

CONFERENCE

Are you ready for the journey of descent? What excites you about that? What scares you?

3. DEPENDENCE

READ

Trust in the LORD with all your heart
and lean not on your own understanding;
in all your ways submit to him,
and he will make your paths straight. (PROV. 3:5-6)

REFLECT

Did you catch the first word from today's text? *Trust.* Dependence is the fruit of trust. Our dissatisfaction often comes from depending on someone or something that is not dependable. In many cases that someone is ourselves (a.k.a. independence). In other cases our broken ways lead us to an unhealthy dependence on others (a.k.a. codependence).

Holy dissatisfaction leads to deeper depths of knowing Jesus, and the more we know Jesus, the more we will trust him—which demonstrates itself in a thousand practical ways of dependence. The old hymn puts it well, "Jesus, Jesus how I trust him, how I've proved him over and over; Jesus, Jesus, precious Jesus, O for grace to trust him more."

The text uses another interesting word: *all,* as in, "with all your heart" and "in all your ways." Dependence takes time. It takes growth. It takes healing. We cannot depend on someone we cannot trust. The way we build trust is to grow bit by bit in our dependence on Jesus. This is where we learn to pray without ceasing (see 1 Thessalonians 5:17). This is the way we learn to lean on Jesus. Growing in dependence on the Holy

Spirit will lead us to a place of surrendering all. This is the place it really gets good.

In order to grow in our dependence, we need a band of brothers or sisters to help us. As our trust in Jesus grows, so will our trust in others grow. In like fashion, as our trust in others grows, our trust in Jesus will grow. The beautiful thing is the way, over time, we will begin to sense Jesus' trust in us.

Dependence is the turning point in this journey of awakening. It will become a well-worn pivot, where the movement from dissatisfaction to satisfaction takes root.

PRAY

Lord Jesus, we can be so quick to believe, yet so slow to trust. And this only reveals to us that we don't believe as much as we think we do. Honestly, Lord, our trust has been broken by others—and that has broken us. Restore our ability to trust—both in you and in others, and make this little band a place where this trust can flourish. I want to depend on you for everything. I'm asking you to show me a simple way I can depend on you for something starting now. In Jesus' name, amen.

CONFERENCE

Where in your life right now are you most dependent on God?

4. DELIGHTED

READ

Trust in the LORD and do good;
dwell in the land and enjoy safe pasture.

Take delight in the LORD,
and he will give you the desires of your heart. (PS. 37:3-4)

REFLECT

Note in today's text the progression from trusting the Lord to taking delight in him. If depending on God is a turning point in the journey, delight is one of the final destinations. To delight in someone is to love them from a deep place of satisfaction with and in them. So often, the life hid with Christ in God gets pitched as a duty-bound life characterized by rigorous discipline to a neverending list of spiritual practices and social responsibilities. That's not it. Jesus teaches us that his "yoke is easy and [his] burden is light" (Matt. 11:30), or as The Message translation renders it, a life characterized by the "unforced rhythms of grace" (see Matthew 11:28–30). Delight is one of those unforced rhythms.

The core calling and commitment of the followers of Jesus is to "'Love the Lord your God with all your heart and with all your soul and with all your mind.' This is the first and greatest commandment. And the second is like it: 'Love your neighbor as yourself'" (Matt. 22:37–39). Again, this can become something of a job description complete with a list of commitments, duties, and responsibilities.

Do we believe this is the way God looks upon us? As a series of commitments, duties, and responsibilities he must manage? No. God takes great delight in his children. Are there commitments, duties, and responsibilities? Sure, but that is to look at the relationship from outside of it. Delight is the reality of the relationship from the inside. To love someone is to be on the inside of the relationship and to take great delight in them. We begin by delighting in God for what he has done for us. We grow to delight in God for what he does in us. We mature to delight in God for what he does through us. We arrive, finally, to delight in God for the sheer delight of who he is.

PRAY

Lord Jesus, forgive me for ever thinking my relationship with you was a burden to bear, when all the while it was an easy yoke. I want to know you more, that I might take great delight in you. Come, Holy Spirit, and fill me with the delight of holy love for the greatness and the goodness of God. In Jesus' name, amen.

CONFERENCE

What does delighting in God look like and mean in your understanding and experience?

5. DEVOTED

READ

Be devoted to one another in love. Honor one another above yourselves. (ROM. 12:10)

REFLECT

It's one thing for a parent to experience the genuine love of their children. It's quite another for a parent to experience the love of their children for one another. If delighting in God is the source of our joy, then our becoming devoted to one another is the source of God's joy. If the journey of the awakening begins with John 3:16: "For God so loved the world that he gave his one and only Son, that whoever believes in him shall not perish but have eternal life," it finds its fulfillment in 1 John 3:16: "This is how we know what love is," the apostle teaches us, "Jesus Christ laid down his life for us. And we ought to lay down our lives for our brothers and sisters."

Remember the greatest command about loving God with all we have? Then there was the rest of it about loving your neighbor as yourself. This is what it means to be an awakened person—one who is growing in an ever-deepening experience of being loved by God (which is the freedom to love oneself), and one who is growing in an ever-deepening expression of loving other people. Because there is no end to the depths of the love of God, there is no end to the depths of the journey of awakening. In fact, this is where it comes full circle.

As we are awakened to the delight of loving God and the devotion to loving our neighbor, we invariably come back into touch with a holy dissatisfaction. It does not take long for our love for others to run thin, which brings us face-to-face with our own deficits. We run into the barriers of our broken ways and realize we are out of our depths. We must grow deeper and toward a greater surrender to God, which, in turn, increases our delight in God, which then nourishes our love for others. Yes, this path keeps on going. Rather than becoming stuck in the ruts of a closed-loop circle, we find ourselves moving in the pattern of the gloriously endless outward spiral of the awakening love of God in Jesus Christ.

PRAY

Heavenly Father, thank you for your amazing love, which saves the world, transforms our lives, and renews all of creation. Your ways are perfect. Open the eyes of my heart to grasp more and more of the holy love of your Son, Jesus Christ. Fill me with your Spirit, that I might boldly love others with this same love. Nothing could be more central to life than this. I am ready to be awakened to all the fullness you share with me and to run this course until I meet you face-to-face. In Jesus' name. amen.

CONFERENCE

What do you think about this journey of awakening? Do you see its inner logic? Does it ring true to your soul?

DISSATISFIED

---

1. ROMANS 7:15-20 (ESV)

READ

For I do not understand my own actions. For I do not do what I want, but I do the very thing I hate. Now if I do what I do not want, I agree with the law, that it is good. So now it is no longer I who do it, but sin that dwells within me. For I know that nothing good dwells in me, that is, in my flesh. For I have the desire to do what is right, but not the ability to carry it out. For I do not do the good I want, but the evil I do not want is what I keep on doing. Now if I do what I do not want, it is no longer I who do it, but sin that dwells within me.

REFLECT

Can we be honest? Can we just call it what it is? We have a problem. There is an ever-present gap between who we aspire to become and who we actually are right now. Can you just say this next sentence out loud? "I want to become more than I presently am." Say it again. Did you hear those words coming out of your mouth? Say it once more, this time with feeling.

Congratulations! Do you realize what you just did? You identified within yourself what we call "holy dissatisfaction." It puts language around the gap between who we know ourselves to be and who we seek to become. When we honestly name this condition in ourselves, we set foot on the path we refer to as the "second half of the gospel." There's the first half of the gospel, which is the process and the crisis of becoming a Christian. Then there's the second half, which is the crisis and the process of, yes, actually becoming a Christian.

Okay, more honesty. This little band you are forming is not your typical accountability group. This is not about holding one another accountable to be better managers of the sin in your life. Today's text is a good description of sin management. The followers of Jesus do not live in Romans 7. Our home is in Romans 8, which begins by saying, "Therefore, there is now no condemnation for those who are in Christ Jesus, because through Christ Jesus the law of the Spirit who gives life has set you free from the law of sin and death" (vv. 1–2).

The gap we feel between who we are and who we want to be is the gap between Romans 7 and Romans 8. The problem for most of us followers of Jesus is we have become trapped in Romans 7. We are caught in the gravity of sin. From here the best we can do is commiserate with other believers about our sin and do our best to be accountable to managing it. The second half of the gospel actually begins with a major shifting of the center of gravity. The new reality of the followers of Jesus is the gravity of the Holy Spirit. This is the place of deliverance from sin's power. This is the place where, in the words of the great poet laureate of Methodism Charles Wesley, "He breaks the power of cancelled sin. He sets the prisoner free."

I know. That's a lot to roll out on a Monday. It will take time, but that's where we are headed. Remember, dissatisfaction can be a good thing, holy even. It can be a doom loop, as in Romans 7, or it can be a doorway into Romans 8.

PRAY

Father, I'm tired of the same old patterns, habits—and yes—ruts in my walk with you. I'm ready to move beyond managing sin and on to real deliverance from it. I want to walk in the light. I want to live free. I want to become the person you imagined when you first made me. Come, Holy Spirit, and make my dissatisfaction with where I am holy and a doorway into a new reality. In Jesus' name, amen.

CONFERENCE

Share together about how you see the difference between sin management and true freedom and life in the power of the Holy Spirit. Share a word that puts courage into your band mates about taking this journey. Be bold.

2. LUKE 24:13-21

READ

Now that same day two of them were going to a village called Emmaus, about seven miles from Jerusalem. They were talking with each other about everything that had happened. As they talked and discussed these things with each other, Jesus himself came up and walked along with them; but they were kept from recognizing him.

He asked them, "What are you discussing together as you walk along?"

They stood still, their faces downcast. One of them, named Cleopas, asked him, "Are you the only one visiting Jerusalem who does not know the things that have happened there in these days?"

"What things?" he asked.

"About Jesus of Nazareth," they replied. "He was a prophet, powerful in word and deed before God and all the people. The chief priests and our rulers handed him over to be sentenced to death, and they crucified him; but we had hoped that he was the one who was going to redeem Israel."

REFLECT

Sometimes the story doesn't go as planned. The dream falls through. They hurt you. The job is lost. The school says no. The success never comes. Where do you go when the story breaks down?

The disciples in this story were disillusioned and disoriented. First the trauma of the crucifixion, and now these rumors of resurrection. It all left them confused and searching for what to do next. They were disoriented by the resurrection because they had not dared to hope for it. They had hoped for something else. They confessed, "but we had hoped that he was the one who was going to redeem Israel" (v. 21).

Perhaps this is why they were headed to Emmaus. Scholars have noted that about two hundred years prior to this, Emmaus was the site of one of Israel's greatest military victories. Led by Judah Maccabee, an underdog collective of Jewish freedom fighters overthrew their oppressors and ushered in one hundred years of independence. Perhaps they thought Jesus would be this kind of leader and bring this kind of peace. Perhaps they were hoping for an uprising to crush Rome, not a crushed leader who would be raised back up.

Where do you run when the story breaks down? When confusion and chaos hit, when you are disappointed and disillusioned, where do you go?

Their reaction was to search out another script. But Jesus uses the grand story of Scripture to show them how the whole thing has been pointing to him. Even in the disorienting chaos, the Author of the story bends every part of it toward redemption. Stop looking for another script.

PRAY

Jesus, you are Author and Protagonist of the story. You bend every part of my story toward redemption. Help me to have eyes that are open and a heart that is burning, enabled to sense and see you present, engaged, and at work in my small part of the narrative. In Jesus' name, amen.

CONFERENCE

Where do you run when the story breaks down?

3. PSALM 51:10-12 (NASB)

READ

Create in me a clean heart, O God,
 and renew a steadfast spirit within me.
Do not cast me away from Your presence
 And do not take Your Holy Spirit from me.
Restore to me the joy of Your salvation
 And sustain me with a willing spirit.

REFLECT

Did you catch those powerful asking verbs in the text?

Create. Renew. Restore. Sustain.

In this instance we see David, a king, who has everything he could possibly need or even want. At the same time, the prayer reveals a deep dissatisfaction he can no longer satiate by serving his fleshly appetites. His dissatisfaction with himself has led him to a kind of holy desperation which will lead to either despair or divine breakthrough. And yes, often it takes a season of despair and at times even depression to bring one to this kind of desperation before God. This powerful king has come to know his own profound limitations. At the same time, he knows a God beyond them.

Create. Renew. Restore. Sustain.

It is so easy to slowly slip into a distracted life that holds a holy dissatisfaction at bay. Though our dissonance be hidden from our awareness, it remains—quietly waiting, all the while pleading for us to wake up to our desperation for God, who alone can create, renew, restore, and sustain.

A few verses earlier we see a key to awakening:

Behold, You desire truth in the innermost being,
And in the hidden part You will make me know wisdom.
(PS. 51:6 NASB)

Holy dissatisfaction means coming to grips with the untruth in our innermost being. The source of our discontent is not external to us. Neither is the solution to our satisfaction. This kind of dissonance is the beautiful sign that God is working within us to touch and transform our innermost being with grace and truth.

This is where the new day begins—in the darkness of dissonance, when our holy dissatisfaction awakens the dawn.

PRAY

Heavenly Father, thank you for desiring truth in my innermost being. Thank you for your patience with me. And thank you for sowing deep within me this holy dissatisfaction at the gap between your desire for me and my desire for you. Yes, Lord, I am awakening to my desire for truth in my innermost being, which is leading me to an even deeper desire for you. Come, Holy Spirit! Create, renew, restore, and sustain us: (name the members of your band). In Jesus' name, amen.

CONFERENCE

How do you relate to this notion of distraction covering over our dissatisfaction and causing us to feed our deepest desires with the things that can never satisfy? Can you see that in your own life? Will you name it? Share this with your band.

Now ask the Holy Spirit to give you a particular word of encouragement for one of the members of your band. Be bold and share that word with the group.

4. EZEKIEL 37:1-5

READ

The hand of the LORD was on me, and he brought me out by the Spirit of the LORD and set me in the middle of a valley; it was full of bones. He led me back and forth among them, and I saw a great many bones on the floor of the valley, bones that were very dry. He asked me, "Son of man, can these bones live?"

I said, "Sovereign LORD, you alone know."

Then he said to me, "Prophesy to these bones and say to them, 'Dry bones, hear the word of the LORD! This is what the Sovereign LORD says to these bones: I will make breath enter you, and you will come to life.'"

REFLECT

Ezekiel was an Old Testament prophet, described in his book as a watchman, commissioned to warn God's people about the judgment coming their way. But they responded as we so often do. They refused to listen to the conviction and wisdom of the

Holy Spirit. Ezekiel was sounding the alarm but they chose to stay asleep.

Then, on August 14, 586 BC, Jerusalem was brutally attacked and the city was destroyed by the Babylonian army. Even the temple was left in ruins. The trauma left Ezekiel the watchman silent for thirteen years. The Holy Spirit finally broke this silence, filling his mouth with hope and opening his eyes to a fresh vision of restoration for God's beloved people.

In chapter 37 he was shown a sprawling valley, littered with dry bones. What he saw was a reflection of what he had experienced. This vision was a projection of the lament and tragedy that scarred his soul.

Perhaps this haunting imagery feels all too familiar. Life is a valley of dry, dead bones—betrayal, addiction, failure, anxiety, loss. All around the landscape is a wasteland of brokenness.

The Spirit asks Ezekiel a provoking question. "Can these bones live?" (v. 3). Ezekiel recalls that, as he was speaking, "there was a noise, a rattling sound" (v. 7).

Death and destruction are reversed and the Holy Spirit breathes vibrant, pulsing life into once empty, dry souls. What Ezekiel sees is a glimpse of the future, a snapshot of the resurrection power of Jesus, washing over the valley of death.

This is our story. This is our reality. What the watchman saw then is waiting for us now. Even as the question echoes in our souls, and we doubt whether our valley is the final scene, there is a noise in the distance. A rattling sound. And even dead bones come awake at his calling.

PRAY

Holy Spirit, we are dry bones apart from your life. Breathe in us again. Shake us awake. Provoke us beyond our discontent and into fresh renewal. Bring healing to our brokenness. We surrender to the life-giving strength of your voice. Let us rise up in you. In Jesus' name, amen.

CONFERENCE

What regrets or failures or brokenness speak with undue authority over you?

What is the Spirit speaking in response?

5. EXODUS 3:1-5

READ

Now Moses was tending the flock of Jethro his father-in-law, the priest of Midian, and he led the flock to the far side of the wilderness and came to Horeb, the mountain of God. There the angel of the LORD appeared to him in flames of fire from within a bush. Moses saw that though the bush was on fire it did not burn up. So Moses thought, "I will go over and see this strange sight—why the bush does not burn up."

When the LORD saw that he had gone over to look, God called to him from within the bush, "Moses! Moses!"

And Moses said, "Here I am."

"Do not come any closer," God said. "Take off your sandals, for the place where you are standing is holy ground."

REFLECT

A season of holy dissatisfaction often culminates in a moment of holy encounter,which leads to an experience of holy intimacy.

In this familiar passage, God commands Moses to take off his sandals, because the very dirt that he is standing on is holy ground. Why does God ask Moses to do this? Obviously, removing his shoes was a sign of respect for the sacred nature of that moment and place. But have you ever considered what happened when Moses took off his shoes? Suddenly, Moses comes in direct, unfiltered contact with the holiness of that ground. The barrier of the sandal is removed and the lowest part of his body is brought into intimate, skin-to-skin contact with God's brilliant purity. Holiness touches him.

It is right for us to view this moment through the lens of calling, where Moses receives clear direction about where he will go and how he will spend the rest of his life. But this breakthrough is about more than clarity. It is also about intimacy.

Perhaps you need the same. In seasons of dissatisfaction we are hungry for a clear word of direction for what to do or where to go next. But maybe God is inviting you to take off your sandals to experience his touch on your life, the skin-to-skin contact of holy intimacy. It is this kind of deeply personal encounter and experience that empowers us to trust the word of direction. It is out of this intimacy that we begin to desire obedience to his command. Not out of fear for punishment, but out of love for him. You might feel like you're wandering in a desert looking for direction from a burning bush. Maybe it's not the bush that needs to be kindled again. Take off your sandals and lean into his touch.

PRAY

God of holy fire, of burning bush and burning heart, rekindle the flame in me. In my wandering, find me. In my discontent, be my longing. Take this desert that looks and feels like a wasteland, and make it holy ground. In Jesus' name, amen.

CONFERENCE

When was the last time you felt the intimate touch of God in your life?

DEEPER

---

1. EPHESIANS 1:3-6

READ

Praise be to the God and Father of our Lord Jesus Christ, who has blessed us in the heavenly realms with every spiritual blessing in Christ. For he chose us in him before the creation of the world to be holy and blameless in his sight. In love he predestined us for adoption to sonship through Jesus Christ, in accordance with his pleasure and will—to the praise of his glorious grace, which he has freely given us in the One he loves.

REFLECT

The direction of deeper is not up.

We all want to go deeper. And we imagine that as we move deeper, the Holy Spirit will set us up on a mountaintop, elevated above the struggle of the world around us. But the direction of deeper is not up. The direction of deeper is down.

These words in Epheisans are inspiring, but Paul knows that enthusiasm alone will never be enough to sustain the life of this church he loves. So he challenges them to remember who they are, even in the thick of the struggle. In this masterful work he is speaking into them and over them who they are in Christ. Their identity is dependent upon Christ's identity. Paul is moving them beyond inspiration and into identity.

These words are not sparked by a sunset over the ocean or a hike up a mountain trail. Most scholars think Paul wrote this letter from behind the bars of a prison cell with the threat of death hanging over his head. And he is not writing to a group of Christians huddled together in a commune, in a monastery, or detached from society. The city of Ephesus was a culturally rich, thriving economic center with competing values that would have been dismissive at times, hostile at others, toward their Christian faith. As far as religious climate, Ephesus was home to the Temple of Artemis, a structure so influential it is considered one of the Seven Wonders of the Ancient World. To live as a light in the shadow of this reality, Paul knew inspiration alone would not be enough. He anchored them in their identity so they would remember that through the struggle.

He extends the same challenge to us. Do you want to go deeper? Then follow Jesus down the mountain into the broken places of the world, where we are rooted in and sustained by the base truth of who we are, our identity in Christ. The direction of deeper is down.

PRAY

Jesus, lead us into the deeper life. We confess that we want this road to lead us into higher places, above the fray. But we declare that we want you more. You are the Pioneer of this downward journey into surrender and burial. And we will follow you. In Jesus' name, amen.

CONFERENCE

Read the text aloud and everywhere the words *we, us,* and *you* appear, insert the names of each person (one after another) in your band, including your own name. This will be powerful, but only if you do it.

2. EPHESIANS 3:14-19

READ

For this reason I kneel before the Father, from whom every family in heaven and on earth derives its name. I pray that out of his glorious riches he may strengthen you with power through his Spirit in your inner being, so that Christ may dwell in your hearts through faith. And I pray that you, being rooted and established in love, may have power, together with all the Lord's holy people, to grasp how wide and long and high and deep is the love of Christ, and to know this love that surpasses knowledge—that you may be filled to the measure of all the fullness of God.

REFLECT

Did you catch those last ten words from today's text? They are the most unfathomable words we could ever imagine as human beings. Go back and read them again. Here they are: "filled to the measure of all the fullness of God."

How can it be possible for you and me to be filled to the measure of all the fullness of God? This is the destination of this movement of the soul we call "deeper." Now, as we've said before, deeper means going downward. Deeper doesn't mean higher. It means lower. But the deeper the cup, the fuller the fullness, right?

So how might this work, being "filled to the measure of all the fullness of God?" Let's look at the text. First, note the scripture is given to us in the form of prayer. The centerpiece is grasping how wide, long, high, and deep is the love of Christ (v. 18). It is one thing to get this as an intellectual concept and even to believe it. That's not the prayer. It is to "grasp" in a different way, a much deeper way, as the text says, to know something beyond knowledge (v. 19). This is at the level of experience yet deeper than feeling.

It happens when God "strengthen[s] you with power through his Spirit in your inner being" (v. 16). We actually need the power of the Father through his Spirit to comprehend the love of God through his Son. He is praying that we, being rooted and established in love, may have power. This is not love as feeling, but love as power. We are getting way past the milk of spiritual nourishment and into the meat of maturing faith now.

One more small and mostly overlooked phrase needs to be pointed out. It's this one: "together with all the Lord's holy people" (v. 18). We cannot do this alone. It will only happen together. No, we don't have to always be together for it to happen, but we must live in a new way of relationship, of being together. That's what banding together is all about.

That's why we are traveling this way together. Depth only happens together.

PRAY

Jesus, empower us to grasp what surpasses knowledge, which can only happen because you have known and grasped us through your all-surpassing love. In Jesus' name, amen.

CONFERENCE TOGETHER

Get a piece of bread or a cookie or a candy bar or, if you are one of those kind of people, get an apple. Note everything you know about whatever it is you are holding and looking at. Now, take a bite out of said piece of food. Note what you know about it. See the difference? Now work this over in light of today's text and reading.

3. COLOSSIANS 2:6-7

READ

So then, just as you received Christ Jesus as Lord, continue to live your lives in him, rooted and built up in him, strengthened in the faith as you were taught, and over-flowing with thankfulness.

REFLECT

Perhaps the most overlooked aspect of today's text are the two words, *as Lord.* In order to "live [our] lives in him," we must receive him "as Lord." We want to believe that growing deeper requires more digging on our part. We need to rev up our devotional engines and shift to a faster gear. We can go on for years dutifully doing our devotions and trying harder to be a better Christian and still be stuck in the same ruts.

What if the path to deeper is not about more Christian activity? What if deeper is about more receptivity? Despite mountains of spiritual activity, our maturing in the Holy Spirit will never exceed the point to which we have "received Christ Jesus as Lord." So how do we do this? It begins with a better question: How do we become this kind of person? This is not about more striving but deeper surrender. The word *Lord* can no longer be a thoughtless word that rolls across our lips. To call someone "Lord" means they have outright ownership of you.

Would you say that "outright ownership" describes your relationship to Jesus? Or is it still kind of fuzzy? The invitation today is to let your knees find a connection with the ground in a new way. Make an ordinary altar—even of the chair you are sitting in—and kneel on the ground at the feet of Jesus. Keep this simple, but make it real. Let something like this come forth from your heart, through your lips, audible enough for your own ears to hear it:

Lord Jesus, you are my Lord. You are my Master. I am yours. I belong to you. Lord Jesus, you are my Lord. I receive you anew and afresh as my Lord.

PRAY

Lord Jesus, you have been many things to me at many times, and yet all of that so often adds up to less than real lordship. Grace me to begin again, but this time with an unqualified, unconditional reception of you as my Lord—yes, as my owner. I confess this is a foreign concept to me, to be owned by someone else. I am sure of it today, though, I want my life to be rooted and built up in you as my Lord. Come, Holy Spirit, and let this kind of faith become my strength. I will be thankful. In your name, Jesus, I pray. Amen.

CONFERENCE

Share with your band a reaction to today's reading. What would it mean to be owned by another person? To be owned by Jesus?

4. ROMANS 12:1-2

READ

Therefore, I urge you, brothers and sisters, in view of God's mercy, to offer your bodies as a living sacrifice, holy and pleasing to God—this is your true and proper worship. Do not conform to the pattern of this world, but be transformed by the renewing of your mind. Then you will be able to test and approve what God's will is—his good, pleasing and perfect will.

REFLECT

You don't start an independent thought with the word *therefore*, unless you enjoy thoroughly confusing your friends. In that case, go for it. Let us know how it works out.

Therefore is used to indicate a continuation, even culmination, of the previous train of thought. When Paul starts this sentence with *therefore*, we understand it is connected to what came before. In fact, scholars say it is connected to *everything* that came before in this letter. This chapter is seen as a hinge point for the entire book, as Paul has been hammering away at the groundbreaking nature of God's extravagant grace. We all have sinned and fallen short of the glory of God and are justified freely according to his grace (see Romans 3:23–24). "While we were still sinners, Christ died for us" (Rom. 5:8). The earned wages of sin is death, but the free gift of God is eternal life through the grace of Jesus Christ (see Romans 6:23). And now, he brings it to the point of response. *Therefore,* in view of this mercy, here is how you should respond: offer your bodies as living sacrifices (see Romans 12:1).

It is strange imagery. Vivid and graphic to the ears of the original audience, he chooses an image that was prominent in both Jewish and pagan forms of worship. The ritual of sacrifice was an agent of keeping or creating peaceful relationship with the deity one worshipped.

But this sacrifice is not an act that makes things right between us and God; Jesus has finished that work, once and for all. It is not a form of paying God back; grace is free and cannot be earned. This sacrifice is simply the only possible response to the breathtaking scope of his mercy—all-out surrender. Surrender so complete and all-encompassing that the only way to depict it is by using the language of death. The way deeper is down. And new life in Jesus only comes on the other side of death to our old selves. To move deeper is to embrace the way of surrender. In view of God's mercy, it is our only possible response.

PRAY

Jesus, you are the once-and-for-all sacrifice. And we surrender our lives to you. Every part of who we are, what we own, what we love— everything about us belongs to you. As we contemplate the depth of your grace, we are in awe. In view of your mercy, we offer ourselves as living sacrifices, holy and pleasing to you. In Jesus' name, amen.

CONFERENCE

How does this imagery of sacrifice strike you? What response does it stir up in you?

5. PHILIPPIANS 2:5-7 (NRSV)

READ

Let the same mind be in you that was in Christ Jesus,
  who, though he was in the form of God,
  did not regard equality with God
  as something to be exploited,
but emptied himself, . . .

REFLECT

Today we come to the master text on this movement of deeper. If I had to reduce the meaning of deeper to one word it would be *descent*. As we will always remind each other, deeper means down.

In today's text we see an unfathomable vision: a God who descends. In today's text we hear an unmistakable calling: become a person who descends. If we remember our story, we will recall this tragic scene in the garden: "For God knows that when you eat from it your eyes will be opened, and you will be like God, knowing good and evil" (Gen. 3:5).

It's right there. The ones created in the image of God decided that equality with God was something to be grasped, and they reached for it. Yet Jesus, the one who was in very nature God, did not consider equality with God something to be grasped.

This movement to grasp for and try to make ourselves something we are not has been with us from the beginning. It's the quest for depth through self-powered and self-oriented ascent. The kingdom of the world runs by this race to the top. The kingdom of heaven moves by this sacred journey to the bottom. The world teaches us to fill ourselves so that we can become more than we are. Jesus teaches us to empty ourselves of all that so we can become who we most truly are.

This is hard work, but it is the real work. Deeper is the work of laying down all of the facades and false selves we have constructed over the building project of our lives. It's yet another reason we must be banded together to get there.

PRAY

Lord Jesus, we can never think thoughts after you until we have your mind in us. We confess, though, that everything in our mind seems to be just opposite of your mind. Awaken us in a new way to understand your ways—to be given to your leadership—and to follow you because, apart from you, we will never find your way. Thank you that you do this so well. For your name's sake, amen.

CONFERENCE

Write a word of encouragement to one or more of your band mates, a specific and personal word, about how you see them taking the lower road to real depth.

WEEK FOUR
DEPENDENT

1. JOHN 15:4-5

READ

Remain in me, as I also remain in you. No branch can bear fruit by itself; it must remain in the vine. Neither can you bear fruit unless you remain in me.

I am the vine; you are the branches. If you remain in me and I in you, you will bear much fruit; apart from me you can do nothing.

REFLECT

The movement of deeper leads us into the graced reality of dependence. Our dependence on Jesus will never exceed the depth of our real relationship with him. How does this work? It's not that we don't want to trust him, it's that our ability to trust has been broken. The work of deepening, or descent, leads us into those broken places and heals our ability to trust. It frees us from the slavery of trying to build up our ability to trust in ourselves or our image or wealth or, on the darker side, our addictions.

In the previous chapter 14 of John, and in the following chapter 16, Jesus is teaching his disciples about the Holy Spirit. Between these chapters he gives us a brilliant picture of what it looks like when people on earth live in abiding trust and dependence on an unseen God who is in heaven. The image of a vineyard overflowing with grapes is the metaphor Jesus chooses to talk about how his disciples must depend on him. This could be some of the clearest and plainest spoken teaching on depending on God in all of the Bible.

Jesus likens himself to the vine, he likens his disciples to the branches, and he likens an abundant harvest of grapes as the outcome of a life lived in trusting and loving dependence on him. The Holy Spirit is the mysterious movement of the power of God through the vine, into the branches, and onward into irresistible fruit.

Here's the kicker: "Apart from me you can do nothing" (v. 5). Okay, the truth is you can do something. It's just that it will amount to nothing.

PRAY

Abba Father, not only are you a good Father but you are a good Farmer. Thank you for your gracious work of pruning in my life. I give you full permission to prune out all my self-dependent and codependent ways. Lead me into the freedom of life in the flow of the Holy Spirit. I want to bear fruit, but I cannot do it apart from you. Teach me this in the depths of my soul. In Jesus' name, amen.

CONFERENCE

Can you name a couple of places in your life where you are really depending on the Holy Spirit right now?

2. ROMANS 8:14-16

READ

For those who are led by the Spirit of God are the children of God. The Spirit you received does not make you slaves, so that you live in fear again; rather, the Spirit you received brought about your adoption to sonship. And by him we cry, "Abba, Father." The Spirit himself testifies with our spirit that we are God's children.

REFLECT

As a dad of five young kids, there seldom is a twenty-minute stretch where I don't hear my kids calling out to me, "Dad" . . . "I need" . . . "Can you" . . . "I'm hungry." It is constant work, constant attention and affection, and constant needs to be met. Our children are completely dependent on us . . . and as they get older, their needs change, but they still depend on us.

Romans 8 is all about the contrast between a person living according to the Spirit, which leads to life (or spiritual life), verses living according to their flesh, which leads to death (or spiritual death). Then it goes on to clarify exactly what living according to the Spirit looks like, and Paul concludes that living in this way looks like a son or daughter depending on a parent. This is more than a mere metaphor, however; instead, Paul is saying, "The Spirit you received," that would be the Holy Spirit you received at conversion, literally adopts you in to a new kind of relationship and teaches you to cry out, "Abba, Father." The Spirit teaches you to depend on our Father for all things.

In 2013, I got dehydrated then lost up on a mountain trail in Haiti, very far from help. I wrestled for a long time with what my strategy would be to get down and back to my group. Ultimately, I decided to do the most humiliating thing I could think of: I yelled at the top of my lungs, "Help!" I kept walking down the mountain under heavy tree cover and every couple of minutes or so I would yell again at the top of my lungs for help. After about fifteen minutes of doing this, I heard someone in the faint distance yelling also. For the next thirty minutes we called out to one another until I was reunited with great relief to my group.

I'm becoming convinced that we do not really come to live according to the Spirit until we are convinced we are not getting out of this mess on our own—whether by choice or by circumstance, we must become desperate enough to call out to God. We must learn to cry out to him and tune our attention to recognize his voice calling back into our souls. In a strange way, we must learn to be more like children calling out to an incredibly attentive parent, "Dad" . . . "I need" . . . "Can you" . . . "I'm hungry." Go ahead, he is listening.

PRAY

Father, we confess our deep need for you. Without you, we are lost. But surrendered and dependent on you, we are fully found. In Jesus' name, amen.

CONFERENCE

Can you name a time in your life where you felt so desperate that praying to God was all you could think to do?

3. ESTHER 4:12-16

READ

When Esther's words were reported to Mordecai, he sent back this answer: "Do not think that because you are in the king's house you alone of all the Jews will escape. For if you remain silent at this time, relief and deliverance for the Jews will arise from another place, but you and your father's family will perish. And who knows but that you have come to your royal position for such a time as this?"

Then Esther sent this reply to Mordecai: "Go, gather together all the Jews who are in Susa, and fast for me. Do not eat or drink for three days, night or day. I and my attendants will fast as you do. When this is done, I will go to the king, even though it is against the law. And if I perish, I perish."

REFLECT

The story of Esther is invasive.

Of course, it's interesting. It's a favorite book of the Bible, yet, strangely, it never mentions God. You can't miss his hand in these pages, but you will not find his name. Beyond interesting, it's inspirational. Generations have drawn courage from the example of Esther. So much so, that Hitler banned this book for fear that it would inspire the rise of another leader like her.

But it is more than interesting or inspiring. The story of Esther is invasive. The Holy Spirit pushes it into our hearts and confronts us with its meaning. He reminds us that none of us have the power to do everything. But when we have the power to do *something*, it is wrong to do nothing.

We are often asked to be the lone ones with small voices, walking into the throne room with borrowed strength because we live by the agenda of another King. You know that feeling, don't you? The one in the pit of your stomach, lump in your throat, sweat on your palms, and heat on your face. Heart racing and tears on the edge of your eyes. There's a word for that feeling. It's called *courage*.

God is crafting an intricate story, unfolding plot twists you never dreamed possible, weaving your story into his sweeping narrative of hope. You have a role. And no one else can play your part. Not because he needs you. It's better than that. He *wants* you.

You can't make your life count; it already does. Will you leverage your small role, small power, small moments for his glory, purpose, and kingdom?

PRAY

God of Esther, ignite a courage in me to speak truth to power, and live truth in the midst of opposition. Help me to raise my voice, even when it shakes. Enable me to speak up for those who have no voice. Help me to depend on you as the source of my strength, because the strength I have is not enough. In Jesus' name, amen.

CONFERENCE

Have you ever found yourself in a moment when you had to depend on God for courage? Share your story with your band.

4. DANIEL 3:16-18

READ

Shadrach, Meshach and Abednego replied to him, "King Nebuchadnezzar, we do not need to defend ourselves before you in this matter. If we are thrown into the blazing furnace, the God we serve is able to deliver us from it, and he will deliver us from Your Majesty's hand. But even if he does not, we want you to know, Your Majesty, that we will not serve your gods or worship the image of gold you have set up."

REFLECT

It takes great faith to believe God can work a miracle. Perhaps it takes greater faith to believe even when he does not.

Shadrach, Meshach, and Abednego are commanded, along with the entire Babylonian Empire, to bow to an image of gold constructed by King Nebuchadnezzar. As the sea of people bow in reverence to the idol, these three young men stand as a tiny band of resistance against the most powerful empire in their world. What gave them the strength to do this? These young men had a vision. They could see an ultimate reality that others could not even imagine, and they staked their very lives on their all-out trust in God.

They were possessed by what Karl Barth called, "the defiant nevertheless"—a surrendered dependence that empowered them to face the flames. Perhaps this is the purest form of faith. This is the true hope of this story. It reveals that, in times of trial, God not only demonstrates his power, but even more, he gives his presence. It is interesting that God does not keep them from the fire; he keeps them *through* it. In the thick of the flames, we are not consumed, because there he is walking with us. And we are reminded that throughout Scripture, fire has been used to represent the intensity of God's presence.

Our God has always been with us in the fire. For Moses, he was in the burning bush and the pillar of fire and cloud. For Elijah, he consumed the offering with fire from heaven. For Isaiah, his presence filled the temple and he promised to see us through the flood and flames. And, of course, at Pentecost our hearts are set ablaze by his Spirit poured out to fill and empower us.

PRAY

God of Shadrach, Meshach, and Abednego, teach me to depend on you. These three young men had no way out unless you made the way. Yet they placed their trust in you. They believed you could perform the miracle, but they were prepared to believe even if you did not. Please cultivate in us "the defiant nevertheless," that surrendered dependence that is not swayed by the prospect of outcome. In Jesus' name, amen.

CONFERENCE

What does it mean to embrace "the defiant nevertheless"? Share a situation in your life that is calling for this scope of reckless surrender.

5. PSALM 18:1-3 (NRSV)

READ

I love you, O Lord, my strength.
The Lord is my rock, my fortress, and my deliverer,
*   my God, my rock in whom I take refuge,*
*   my shield, and the horn of my salvation, my*
*   stronghold.*
I call upon the Lord, who is worthy to be praised,
*   so I shall be saved from my enemies.*

REFLECT

This song of praise, Psalm 18, was David's response to God after Saul and his men had just chased David and his men around a mountain. Just as Saul and his army were surrounding David, Saul received word that the Philistines had made a raid on the land and turned back. David then named that place the "Rock of Escape" (see 1 Samuel 23:25–28).

It's from this place we see that David is declaring that, in fact, God is the rock. He delivered them literally from death. In the story it was a giant rock they were running for their lives on, and here David is declaring, "The LORD is my rock." It was not David's six hundred men who shielded him from Saul; rather, it was the Lord. It isn't the rock they were hiding on; it is God he takes refuge in. It was not the "horn of salvation" or "Rock of Escape" (which both refer to the mountain) he puts his trust in; it is the God who made the mountains who is worthy to be praised.

When David heard Saul was after him, he did not turn first to his trusted men to seek counsel, he prayed and asked God what he should do. So often when we find ourselves in difficult situations we first turn to one of two places most instinctively: ourselves and others. When we turn to ourselves, we must recognize that while we sometimes have accurate instincts and some experience and understanding, we can often get it wrong. Second, while seeking out others can be very helpful, we must consider why we would often rely first on a source that could give uninformed advice or make false assumptions, verses seeking out the God who knows all, sees all, and is over all.

We must come to depend on the reality that God alone is the unshakable rock on which we stand. That he alone is the refuge and shield in the storms and battles of life. This does not mean we are to go about life alone! It is rather the order of things. What if we first turned to God in prayer at the outset of trouble, then sought out the counsel of our band or trusted friend, then made the best decision we could from that vantage point? Perhaps then when things turned around for the better we would pour out our praise first to God rather than patting ourselves on the back. This is how dependence gives way to delight.

There is an old adage, "When the going gets tough, the tough get going." I think a better phrase would be, "When the going gets tough, the tough get praying."

PRAY

Lord, I echo this ancient prayer today: I love you, O Lord, my strength. You are my rock, my fortress, and my deliverer, my God, my rock in whom I take refuge, my shield, and the horn of my salvation, my stronghold. I call upon you, Lord, who is worthy to be praised, so I shall be saved from my enemies. In Jesus' name, amen.

CONFERENCE

Have you ever had an experience in your life where you felt like God clearly answered your prayer in a tough situation? Describe it.

DELIGHTED

1. REVELATION 22:8-9

READ

I, John, am the one who heard and saw these things. And when I had heard and seen them, I fell down to worship at the feet of the angel who had been showing them to me. But he said to me, "Don't do that! I am a fellow servant with you and with your fellow prophets and with all who keep the words of this scroll. Worship God!"

REFLECT

Have you ever been around someone of extraordinary prominence? Perhaps they were extremely wealthy, or famous, an athlete, or held a position of power. Sometimes we can be tempted in the presence of greatness to almost bow down to them or feel unworthy compared to them. There can often be a fine line between showing respect and admiration for someone like this, verses actually placing them on a level of prominence where we cease to see that this is a person, just like us. In fact, they deserve no more dignity than we ourselves or anyone else, because, in fact, God created them, just as he did you. Actor and comedian Jim Carrey once said, "I think everybody should get rich and famous and do everything they ever dreamed of so they can see that it's not the answer." I think an honest statement like this speaks to what I am saying here. After you "arrive" at fame and fortune, you realize that what you had so often looked up to was ultimately not fulfilling what you had been longing for and looking up to.

In this passage in Revelation, John, at the end of an extraordinary vision in the very last chapter of our Bible, reveals that in his ignorance he made a huge error. He fell to the ground and worshipped an angel. The angel rebuked him and said, "I am a fellow servant." In other words, I am created by God just like you, and I serve the same God you do, therefore, don't you do that. Worship God, and God only.

Now step back and consider this. Here a powerful being, showing John an unbelievable vision of all that is and will be in this world, is not worthy of worship. Compare this angel to the greatest man or woman on the planet and the angel seems greater still, don't you think? Yet, the angel warns, "Don't do that!" Don't bow down and worship another fellow servant; worship God.

How often do we find ourselves taking delight in God's creation over taking delight in God himself? We must learn with sober judgment to discern our appetites. What is it, or who is it, that we take delight in more than God? We must recognize that we are so easily carried away to place our delight in something or someone—"Don't do that!" Instead, as A. W. Tozer said, "We must never rest until everything inside us worships God."

PRAY

Almighty God, you are above all things. We worship you and lay all we are on the altar before you. We exalt you because you alone are worthy of our praise. We cannot stand beneath the weight of your glory. So we hit our knees and lift you up. In Jesus' name, amen.

CONFERENCE

What are you most prone to give your delight to other than God? Can you name it honestly and confess that to God today?

2. PSALM 34:1-8 (NASB)

READ

I will bless the LORD at all times;
His praise shall continually be in my mouth.
My soul will make its boast in the LORD;
The humble will hear it and rejoice.
O magnify the LORD with me,
And let us exalt His name together.

I sought the LORD, and He answered me,
And delivered me from all my fears.
They looked to Him and were radiant,
And their faces will never be ashamed.

*This poor man cried, and the L**ORD** heard him*
And saved him out of all his troubles.
*The angel of the L**ORD** encamps around those who*
  fear Him,
And rescues them.

O taste and see that the Lord is good;
How blessed is the man who takes refuge in Him!

REFLECT

The psalmist illuminates the pathway from depending on the Lord to delighting in him. Look at verse 4: "I sought the L**ORD**, and He answered me, and delivered me from all my fears." Dependence leads to deliverance, which leads a person to say things like, "O magnify the L**ORD** with me, And let us exalt His name together" (v. 3).

Remember what Mary said after the angel visited her with the news of what was to come? "My soul magnifies the Lord, and my spirit rejoices in God my Savior" (Luke 1:45 N**RSV**). She delighted in God.

To delight in the Lord is to move toward the place of unquenchable joy. Yes, to delight in God is to enjoy God. Have you ever consciously let yourself enjoy the goodness and glory of God? Note how the psalmist just can't stop. We have blessed the Lord, boasted in the Lord, magnified the Lord, exulted in the Lord, and now this: "O taste and see that the L**ORD** is good" (Ps. 34:8).

Think about the way we take delight in choice foods. I recently found myself in a long line at the drive-through window at Krispy Kreme Donuts. I was so looking forward to one of those freshly cooked hot donuts. I anticipated it with every inch my car moved forward. Finally to the window, I paid and, before they could give me my receipt, I was already biting into one. It was pure delight. Delight is an all-five-senses experience. That's what God wants for us. In fact, this is the way he feels about us.

PRAY

Heavenly Father, if I'm honest, I don't know this experience the psalmist describes. I want to. Would you change the nature and character of my relationship with you such that I can learn to live in this place of delighting in you? Lead me in this way. I know you are good, but I want more. I want to taste and see that you are good. I want to enjoy your goodness. I pray in Jesus' name, amen.

CONFERENCE

Is delighting yourself in the Lord a new experience for you? How does the invitation to do so stretch you? What has delighting in the Lord been like in your experience? How did you do it? Share with your band.

3. JOHN 12:1-8

READ

Six days before the Passover, Jesus came to Bethany, where Lazarus lived, whom Jesus had raised from the dead. Here a dinner was given in Jesus' honor. Martha served, while

Lazarus was among those reclining at the table with him. Then Mary took about a pint of pure nard, an expensive perfume; she poured it on Jesus' feet and wiped his feet with her hair. And the house was filled with the fragrance of the perfume.

But one of his disciples, Judas Iscariot, who was later to betray him, objected, "Why wasn't this perfume sold and the money given to the poor? It was worth a year's wages." He did not say this because he cared about the poor but because he was a thief; as keeper of the money bag, he used to help himself to what was put into it.

"Leave her alone," Jesus replied. "It was intended that she should save this perfume for the day of my burial. You will always have the poor among you, but you will not always have me."

REFLECT

This is the shocking, self-emptying nature of profound love. In this small frame we see a prophetic echo of how God loves us, as well as a prototype for how to love God—broken and poured out, in full abandon. It's a scene that does not add up.

Foreshadowing the sacrifice of Jesus mere days away, Mary breaks open her most expensive gift (a sign of his death) and anoints him (a burial ritual he will not be afforded between the cross and tomb). The potent aroma of extravagant love fills the room. Mary beholds the treasure in front of her, and empties her treasure at his feet.

Meanwhile, Judas is doing the math. And his calculations are off. Livid over this undignified and wasteful display, he masks his true intentions behind the vestments of stewardship. Why does Jesus trust the money bag to the thief? It's not about how much trust Jesus had in Judas, but how much trust he placed in money. He knew it's power to steal our affection, it's way of making us miss the treasure. Yes, Judas did his math and ran the numbers. And, in the end, he sold the treasure of heaven for thirty pieces of silver.

In "Manifesto: The Mad Farmer Liberation Front," the farmer and poet Wendell Berry wrote, "every day do something that won't compute." This is the call of kingdom accounting, the great exchange, the vision to behold the treasure hidden right before our eyes. It challenges us with the provocative question: "What is he worth to you?"

PRAY

Jesus, you are the Treasure of heaven, broken and poured out in extravagant love. Help me to live a life in reckless response, a life that does not compute. May it look like a waste to some and like worship to you. In Jesus' name, amen.

CONFERENCE

Identify the competing priorities in your life which threaten to steal your affection or attention. How can you recalculate and actively behold the Treasure and live out the extravagant exchange?

4. 2 SAMUEL 6:12-15

READ

Now King David was told, "The LORD *has blessed the household of Obed-Edom and everything he has, because of the ark of God." So David went to bring up the ark of God from the house of Obed-Edom to the City of David with rejoicing. When those who were carrying the ark of the* LORD *had taken six steps, he sacrificed a bull and a fattened calf. Wearing a linen ephod, David was dancing before the* LORD *with all his might, while he and all Israel were bringing up the ark of the* LORD *with shouts and the sound of trumpets.*

REFLECT

Recently, at a New Room Conference, we had Bishop James Edward Swanson Sr. preach. It was the first time in my life that I had ever seen a preacher dance a lap around the auditorium, praising God at the top of his lungs, to end his sermon. Some might have thought this display was over-the-top or even undignified. For me, it reminded me of King David's rejoicing and dancing before the Lord with all his might while bringing the Ark of the Lord into the City of David.

In David, we see a strong leader, whom many believed should maintain a calm and controlled demeanor before his people. This was accentuated by Michal, daughter of Saul, who chastised David for his dancing and suggested that it was indecent to be seen in this way. Then, of course, we have David's famed response, *"I will celebrate before the* Lord. *I will become even more undignified than this, and I will be humiliated in my own eyes"* (2 Sam. 6:21–22, emphasis mine).

Interestingly, we could contrast this passage with the words of Jesus who said, "But when you pray, go into your room, close the door and pray to your Father, who is unseen. Then your Father, who sees what is done in secret, will reward you" (Matt. 6:6). It would appear that Scripture encourages both secret acts of prayer and praise along with public acts. Matthew Henry clarifies this when he said, "As secret worship is better the more secret it is, so public worship is better the more public it is." Perhaps we should take our cue from David and Bishop Swanson: if we are going to delight in God publicly, we should do it with all our hearts, like we mean it. If we are to delight in God privately, we should do it with all our hearts in secret, like we mean it.

PRAY

Jesus, you are the Most High King. I worship you from the bottom of my heart, from the secret of my room to the top of my lungs. In Jesus' name, amen.

CONFERENCE

Can you recall a time in your life when you worshipped God with everything you had in secret? Now what about publicly? Consider sharing one or both of these with your band.

5. MATTHEW 22:34-40

READ

Hearing that Jesus had silenced the Sadducees, the Pharisees got together. One of them, an expert in the law, tested him with this question: "Teacher, which is the greatest commandment in the Law?"

Jesus replied: "'Love the Lord your God with all your heart and with all your soul and with all your mind.' This is the first and greatest commandment. And the second is like it: 'Love your neighbor as yourself.' All the Law and the Prophets hang on these two commandments."

REFLECT

The religious experts once again set a trap for Jesus. And, again, he does more than slip past it. He uses their web to untangle the truth, revealing the hypocrisy of their religious legalism and the freedom of his redeeming love.

It takes a sharp mind to grasp the vast, complex nuances of the Jewish law. It takes a brilliant mind to simplify all of that information into one core thought that somehow encompasses the entire thing. Complexity leads to confusion. Simplicity leads to revelation. That's exactly what happens in this passage.

Technically speaking, Jesus doesn't choose just one command. He combines two. Has that ever bothered you? Isn't this cheating? Does he think he can get away with it because he is Jesus? No. He is showing us that these two together create one complete command. You cannot separate the two.

It's like this: Which is more important, breathing in or breathing out? Pick one. Of course, you can't pick one. Breathing requires both. In fact, if you aren't doing both, then pretty soon, you'll be doing neither.

The same is true with this command. If you aren't doing both, you are doing neither. Love for God that produces a love for others is Christian breathing. And without breathing, there can be no life. Throughout this journey we've talked about coming awake. But perhaps without grasping this we have yet to come alive.

This is the Jesus way, truth, and life—to love God with all we have and all we are. And as our hearts turn outward toward him, he will train us to love others in the same reckless and ridiculous way.

PRAY

Jesus, teach us the most simple way—to love you and those you love. Empower us to grasp the depth of this understanding, seeing everything we do through the lens of fulfilling this law, because it's already fulfilled in you. Reshape the curvature of our hearts, turning them outward through your love for us, to love you and others. Call us to wake up and come alive in your love, which is the ground and source of every living thing. In Jesus' name, amen.

CONFERENCE

What is one obstacle to loving the people in your life? We're not talking about theoretical groups of people that are out there somewhere. But your family, friends, coworkers, band mates.

DEVOTED

---

1. LUKE 4:16-21

READ

He went to Nazareth, where he had been brought up, and on the Sabbath day he went into the synagogue, as was his custom. He stood up to read, and the scroll of the prophet Isaiah was handed to him. Unrolling it, he found the place where it is written:

"The Spirit of the Lord is on me,
because he has anointed me
to proclaim good news to the poor.
He has sent me to proclaim freedom for the prisoners
and recovery of sight for the blind,
to set the oppressed free,
to proclaim the year of the Lord's favor."

Then he rolled up the scroll, gave it back to the attendant and sat down. The eyes of everyone in the synagogue were fastened on him. He began by saying to them, "Today this scripture is fulfilled in your hearing."

REFLECT

This is what biblical scholars refer to as a "mic drop moment." Okay, maybe they don't. But they should.

In his hometown synagogue, Jesus announces the launch of his ministry and frames the scope of his mission by reading from Isaiah 61. To the shock of the crowd, he offers a one-line commentary on this beloved passage. He declares that the hope buried in this prophecy has finally been fulfilled through him, right before their eyes.

Many scholars think (for real this time) that the phrase, "the year of the Lord's favor," referred to the ancient practice of the Year of Jubilee. According to the Jewish law, the Jubilee was a sort of hyper-Sabbath year, set to occur once every fifty years. To observe the Jubilee, the people were commanded to release all of their slaves, remove all debt they were owed, and return all land to those who were forced to sell because of financial hardship. Because of the Jubilee rhythm, every Israelite was endowed with an ongoing sense of hope that freedom was always on the horizon. When hardship struck, oppression and poverty would not be their permanent reality, and slavery would not be their unshakable future. It was designed so that most everyone would experience it once in their lifetime.

There was only one problem. It never happened. Historians cannot find evidence that it was ever fully practiced and put into effect by the people because it was simply too difficult to carry out and those who owned the slaves, resources, and property were not willing to let them go. Jubilee was a promise left unfulfilled.

Until, of course, the day that Jesus shows up and announces that the year of the Lord's favor has finally arrived. He is the Jubilee. He is freedom from slavery, and release from oppression, and sight for the blind, and good news for the poor. And, as his people in the world, he commands and empowers us to be the same.

PRAY

Jesus, may your jubilee be unleashed through us. May our churches and our lives become good news for the poor and release for the captives. May the blind see you through us. In Jesus' name, amen.

CONFERENCE

What would it look like if Jesus brought jubilee through you? How would that affect your family? Your work place? Your community? Is your life freedom and release and good news?

2. COLOSSIANS 3:12-17

READ

Therefore, as God's chosen people, holy and dearly loved, clothe yourselves with compassion, kindness, humility, gentleness and patience. Bear with each other and forgive one another if any of you has a grievance against someone. Forgive as the Lord forgave you. And over all these virtues put on love, which binds them all together in perfect unity.

Let the peace of Christ rule in your hearts, since as members of one body you were called to peace. And be thankful. Let the message of Christ dwell among you richly as you teach and admonish one another with all wisdom through psalms, hymns, and songs from the Spirit, singing to God with gratitude in your hearts. And whatever you do, whether in word or deed, do it all in the name of the Lord Jesus, giving thanks to God the Father through him.

REFLECT

The journey from dissatisfied to devoted is marked by transformation. The scandalous grace of Jesus changes our legal standing before God's judgment seat. But it changes more than that. It goes on from glory to glory, cultivating renewal in our hearts, minds, souls, and lives in every conceivable way as we are made new through him. The heart of sin that was turned inward on itself is reoriented and redirected outward toward God and others.

Jesus must be our first love. But he refuses to be our last. He maintains that a profound love for God will produce, by nature of its object, an ever-increasing love for others. And the presence of his Spirit within us will plant, nurture, and produce the first fruit of his own character, namely love.

This is not merely the message of Jesus, but the inherited heartbeat of Paul, and the binding commonality that holds together the communion of the saints. "And over all these virtues," Paul says, "put on love, which binds them together in perfect unity" (v. 14). The term *binds* is used in other places to speak of the ligaments of the body—the part that holds together the infrastructure of our lives. The ligaments serve the purpose of both enabling and restricting movement. They set the parameters for how the body can move and for what the body is not capable of doing. Love empowers certain actions and attitudes, and at the same time, will not allow us to indulge in others. Love is the scope and movement of our lives.

PRAY

Jesus, make your love for us into love for you and others. Enable actions of compassion, kindness, humility, gentleness, and patience. And restrict reactions of arrogance, coldness, harshness, and indifference. Let your peace rule in our hearts. In Jesus' name, amen.

CONFERENCE

What actions has love empowered that are not natural to you? Likewise, what natural reactions has love restricted?

3. 1 CORINTHIANS 13:4-7

READ

Love is patient, love is kind. It does not envy, it does not boast, it is not proud. It does not dishonor others, it is not self-seeking, it is not easily angered, it keeps no record of wrongs. Love does not delight in evil but rejoices with the truth. It always protects, always trusts, always hopes, always perseveres.

REFLECT

Love is not a soft feeling. Love is the hardest thing in the world. In fact, apart from the working of the Holy Spirit in our innermost self, love, as envisioned in Scripture, is impossible.

Try this exercise. Go back and reread today's text aloud, and everywhere you see the word *love* (or its pronoun), insert your name.

How did that impact you? Now go back and read it aloud one more time, only this time insert the name of Jesus.

The point of this exercise is not to get you to compare yourself to Jesus, but to realize that your only hope of becoming a person of real love is Jesus in you. Scripture speaks of this elsewhere as, "Christ in you, the hope of glory" (Col. 1:27).

This is what waking up is all about. It means becoming fully alive to the power of God, which is the love of Jesus Christ, more and more with every passing day. The realization of the gap between where we are and who we aspire to become leads us back through the path of awakening again and again. Holy dissatisfaction with our present capacity to love others leads us deeper into the depths of the mind of Christ, which takes us to new levels of dependence on his presence within us. This leads us to new heights of delighting in God and onward into heretofore unknown possibilities and capacities to love other people.

PRAY

Abba Father, your will is right, your ways are true, and your love is better than life. We want our love for others to become less limited by our deficiencies and more filled with your possibilities. We know this will make us people of arresting character and people whose lives reveal your incredible goodness to others. Lord Jesus, increase our sensitivity to your power, which is love. Raise our awareness of our own deficit of power, which is our lovelessness. Reveal to our innermost self the futility of striving after this in our own strength and lead us in the way of a deeper surrender to you. You have given yourself to us. Now grace us with the courage to give ourselves more fully to you, that you might make us a gift of your love to others. Come, Holy Spirit, and make it so. In Jesus' name, amen.

CONFERENCE

Share together about your own experience of the difference between striving harder and surrendering more deeply.

4. GALATIANS 5:22-26

READ

But the fruit of the Spirit is love, joy, peace, forbearance, kindness, goodness, faithfulness, gentleness and self-control. Against such things there is no law. Those who belong to Christ Jesus have crucified the flesh with its passions and desires. Since we live by the Spirit, let us keep in step with the Spirit. Let us not become conceited, provoking and envying each other.

REFLECT

When we are filled with the Spirit, we receive gifts of the Spirit. These gifts are diverse and given with true power for the building of the church and the advancement of the kingdom. Are you operating in the supernatural gifting of the Holy Spirit? Have you discovered the unique convergence of your gifts and passions, awakened to new strength and effect through the Spirit?

When we are rooted in the Father, connected to Christ and filled with the Holy Spirit, Paul tells us that we will bear the fruit of the Spirit. The branches display the character of the tree. Paul clearly says that we will not all receive every gift of the Spirit, but we should all expect and display every fruit of the Spirit. This is the true sign that his life pulses within us, and is making its way out of us and into the world. Have you ever seen a field in winter? Or orchard or garden? To the eye it looks dead, but we know it is merely asleep. Then, in due season, it is stirring to see sprouts of green in those plots of dirt. And small buds on the branches. And gardens coming awake again. The same happens in us. We begin to show the signs of fruit as the Holy Spirit awakens us to become who he has aspired for us to be.

And it is not by chance that the first fruit listed is love. In fact, love is the seed of every fruit that follows. It is the root command and the core of God's character, cultivated in us. Every other fruit is an aspect of love, expressed through tangible actions and attitudes toward God and others. Martin Luther defined sin as the heart turned inward on itself. John Wesley later defined holiness as the heart turned outward to God and others. This is the journey that begins with holy dissatisfaction and culminates in holy devotion to others around us. It is by no means the source of our salvation, but it is by all means the logical outcome for every disciple walking with obedience in the way of Jesus. *Sola Sanctus Caritas.*

PRAY

Holy Spirit, cultivate your gifts and your fruit in our everyday lives. May the world see you by what they see in us. Keep us rooted so that you may produce in us a harvest for the kingdom. In Jesus' name, amen.

CONFERENCE

What fruit of the Spirit is most clearly seen in your life? Which needs to be nurtured? Share with your band. Then, call out the fruit you see in each other.

5. 1 JOHN 3:14-15

READ

We know that we have passed from death to life, because we love each other. Anyone who does not love remains in death. Anyone who hates a brother or sister is a murderer, and you know that no murderer has eternal life residing in him.

REFLECT

Do you know what a litmus test is? Simply, a litmus test is a chemistry experiment designed to show you if liquid contains acid. It is conducted by taking a strip of litmus paper and dipping it into the liquid to be tested. Based on the presence of acidity, blue litmus paper will turn red and red litmus paper will turn blue, or something like that. (Forgive my middle-aged memory of my eighth-grade chemistry lab.)

John gives us a litmus test on whether a person is a true believer in Jesus Christ:

> *We know that we have passed from death to life, because we love each other. (v. 14)*

We can say we believe in God all day long and deceive ourselves. There is only one way to know. It is the litmus test for the presence of the life of God in our lives. Do we love each other? No one makes this clearer than John:

> *Dear friends, let us love one another, for love comes from God. Everyone who loves has been born of God and knows God. Whoever does not love does not know God, because God is love. (1 John 4:7–8)*

Because John loves us, he is being brutally honest with us. He knows our propensity for self-deception is high. He wants us to wake up and smell the coffee. The litmus test of our relationship with God is our relationships with others.

This is not about having perfect relationships with everyone we know. It is about becoming gut-level honest with ourselves in the presence of God about the quality of the character of our love for others. Is our love becoming less self-interested and more others oriented? The answer to this question will tell us everything we need to know about the depth of our relationship with God and the maturity of our faith.

PRAY

Abba Father, I want to love like you love. I know that my love for others will never exceed my knowing of your love for me. I simply cannot love others as I love myself until my love for myself is founded in your love for me. Open my mind and heart to perceive this love. This will be my freedom and my generosity and my joy. Come, Holy Spirit, and stir this deeper awareness of the brokenness of my love that I might awaken to the wholeness of your love for me. You love me perfectly, unconditionally, and unfathomably. In Jesus' name, amen.

CONFERENCE

Where is your love for others most tested at this moment? What does this tell you about your relationship with Jesus? What is a next step?

the discipleship band meeting structure

The weekly band meeting is simple in structure and format. Budget for twenty minutes per person. Some small talk is fine, but the band must respect the time allotment. The meeting should be formally opened with the words below. Once this happens, it's band business to the end.

I. OPENING

One Voice: Awake O Sleeper and Rise from the Dead.
All Others: And Christ Will Shine on You.

(adapted from Ephesians 4:14)

PRAYER READ IN UNISON OR BY ONE MEMBER OF THE BAND

Heavenly Father, we pray that out of your glorious riches you would strengthen us with power through your Spirit in our inner being, so that Christ may dwell in our hearts through faith. And we pray that we, being rooted and established in love, may have power, together with all the Lord's holy people, to grasp how wide and long and high and deep is the love of Christ, and to know this love that surpasses knowledge—that we may be filled to the measure of all the fullness of God. We ask this in Jesus' name, amen.

(adapted from Ephesians 3:16–19)

II. THE QUESTIONS

1. How is it with your soul?
2. What are your struggles?
3. Any sin to confess?
4. Anything you want to keep secret?
5. How might the Holy Spirit be speaking and moving in your life?

In the interest of keeping it simple and memorable, think of the questions as: Soul, Struggles, Sin, Secrets, Spirit.

At the conclusion of each person's time of sharing, someone from the band will offer a prayer for the one who shared. This is also an opportunity to seek clarification, offer encouragement, and to speak into one another's lives.

It may be advisable for a new band, particularly among people unfamiliar with one another, for the first month to cover question #1 only. Perhaps add question #2 for the second month. Go at your own pace and pay attention to relational dynamics. Focus on building trust and always maintain confidentiality.

III. CLOSING

Now to him who is able to do immeasurably more than all we ask or imagine, according to his power that is at work within us, to him be glory in the church and in Christ Jesus throughout all generations, for ever and ever! Amen.

(Ephesians 3:20–21)

www.ingramcontent.com/pod-product-compliance
Ingram Content Group UK Ltd.
Pitfield, Milton Keynes, MK11 3LW, UK
UKHW020709070726
13597UKWH00019B/133